T0065478

COLOR ME
CHRISTIAN ARTWORK

Art Bratcher

WESTBOW
PRESS®
A DIVISION OF THOMAS NELSON
& ZONDERVAN

WestBow Press books may be ordered through booksellers or by contacting:

WestBow Press
A Division of Thomas Nelson & Zondervan
1663 Liberty Drive
Bloomington, IN 47403
www.westbowpress.com
844-714-3454

Scripture taken from the King James Version of the Bible.

ISBN: 978-1-6642-3605-9 (sc)
ISBN: 978-1-6642-3606-6 (e)

Print information available on the last page.

WestBow Press rev. date: 05/27/2021

"But the very hairs
of your head
are all numbered."

Matthew 10:30

"Thou didst cause judgement to be heard from Heaven; the earth feared, and was still."

Psalm 76:8

"Hear, O Lord,
And have Mercy upon
me:
Lord, be thou my helper."

Psalm 30:10

"So shall I keep thy law continually for ever and ever."

Psalm 119:44

"She will do him good
and not evil all the days
of her life."

Proverb 31:12

"Two are better than one : because the have a good reward for their labour."

Ecclesiastes 4:9

"I cried unto God with
my voice.
Even unto God with my voice
and he gave ear
unto me."

Psalm 77:1

"Thou art more glorious and excellent than the Mountains of prey."

Psalm 76:4

"Man did eat angels`
food:
he sent them meat
to the full."

Psalm 78:25

"But his delight is
in the law of the Lord:
and in his law doth
he meditate day
and night,"

Psalm 1:2

11 Chronicles 15:7

"Be ye strong
therefore,and let not
your hands be weak:
for your works shall
be rewarded."

Matthew 11:30

"For my yoke is
easy,
and my burden
is light."

"Nay, in all these things we are more than conquerors through him that loved us."

Romans 8:37

"Now there are
diversities of gifts,
But the same
spirit."

12:4 1 corinthians

"For he shall deliver
the needy when he crieth;
the poor also,
and him that hath
no helper."

Psalm 72:12

"Do all things without murmurings and disputings:"

Philippians 2:14

"And I, if
I be lifted up
from the earth,
will draw
all men unto me."

John 12:32

"Lord, all my desire
is before thee,
and my groaning
is not hid from
thee."

Psalm 38:9

"And all flesh shall see the salvation of God."

Luke 3:6

"For with thee is
the fountain of life:
in thy light shall
we see light."

Psalm 36:9

"Preserve me, O God:
for in thee do
I put my
trust."

Psalm 16:1

"Give ears to my words,
O Lord, consider my
meditation."

Psalm 5:1

Hebrew
6:14
"Saying,
surely blessing
I will bless thee,
and multiplying
I will multiply thee."

"Every word of God
is pure:
He is a shield unto
that put their
trust in him."

Proverb 30:5

"Now faith is the substance of things hoped for the evidence of things not seen."

Hebrew 11:1

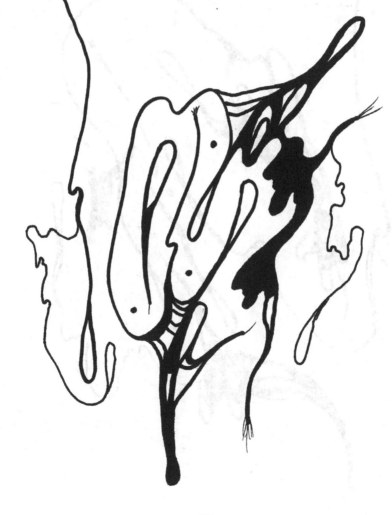

"Come unto me,
all ye that labour and
are heavy laden,
and I will give you rest."

Matthew 11:28

"Be of good courage
and he shall strengthen your
heart, all ye that hope in
the Lord."

Psalm31:24

"This is the day which the
Lord hath made;
we will rejoice and be
glad in it."

Psalm 118:24

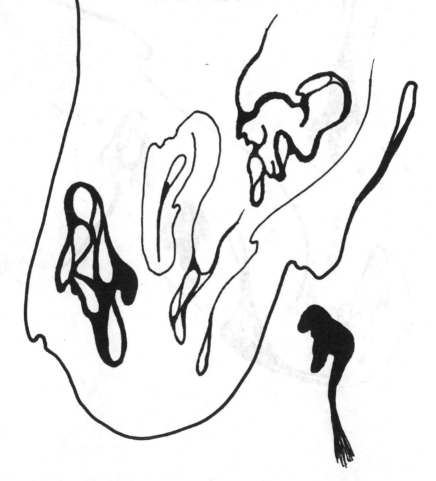

"Rejoice in the Lord
always:
And again I say
rejoice."

Philippians 4:4

"Rejoicing in hope;
patient in tribulation;
continuing in start
in prayer."

Romans 12:12

"Rejoice with them that
do rejoice,
and weep with them that
weep."

Romans 12:15

"That I may come unto you
with joy by the will of God,
and may with you
be refreshed."

Romans 15:32

"These things have I spoken
unto you,
that my joy might remain in you,
and that your Joy might be full."

John 15:11

"I have no greater joy than to hear that my children walk in truth."

3 John 1:4

"Day unto day uttereth speech,
and night unto night sheweth knowledge."

Psalm 19:2

"And he brought forth his people with joy, and his chosen with gladness."

Psalm 105:43

"I laid me down and slept;
I awakened;
For the Lord
sustained me."

Psalm 3:5

"But our God is in the
heavens:
He hath done
whatsoever
he hath pleased."

Psalm 115: 3

"I laid me down and
slept:
I awakened for the Lord
sustained me."

Psalm 3:5

"Give ear to my words,
O Lord.
Consider my
meditation"

Psalm 5:1

"But godliness with contentment is great gain."

1 Timothy 6:6

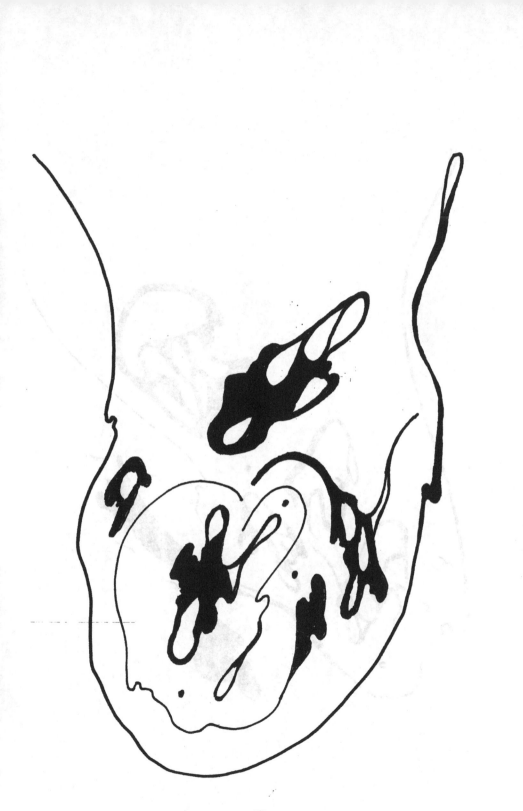

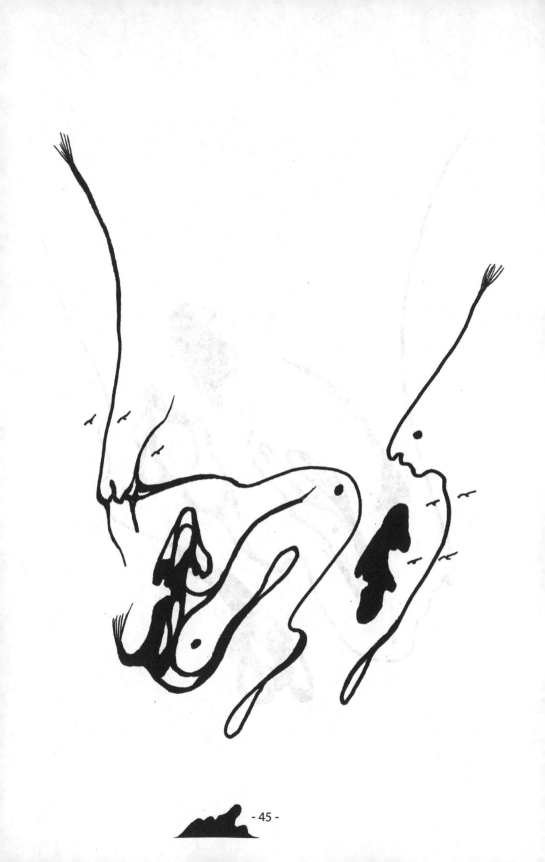

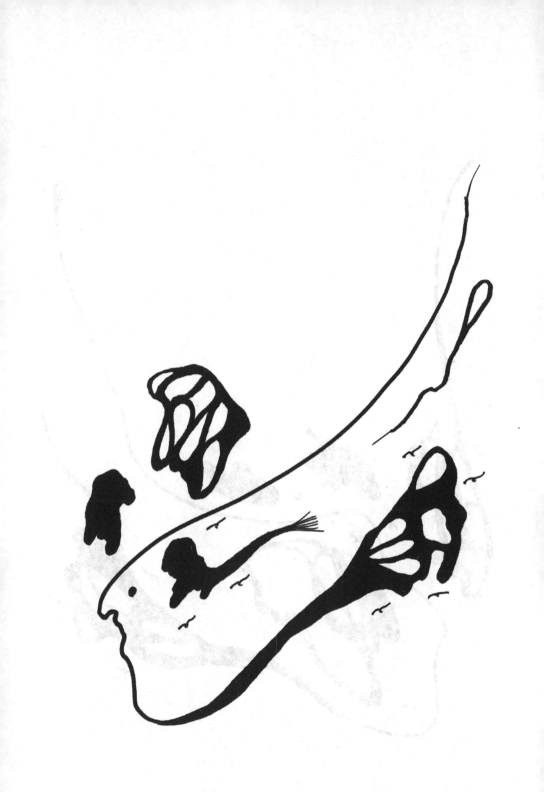

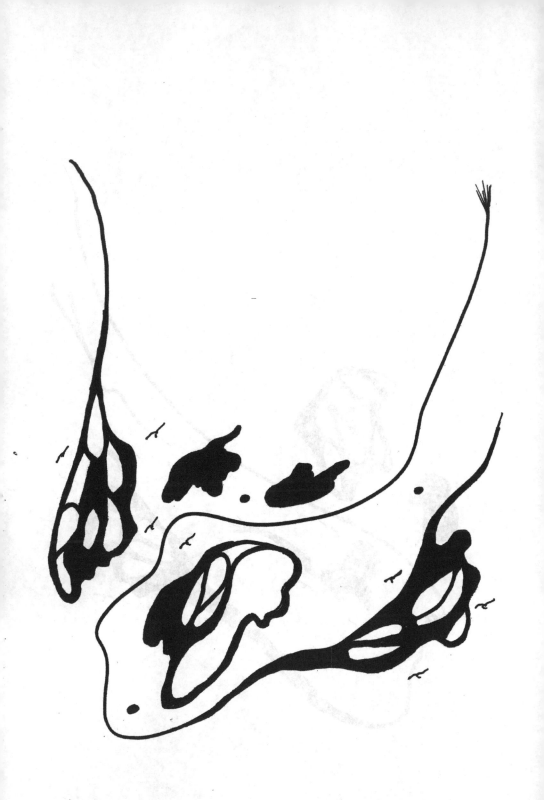

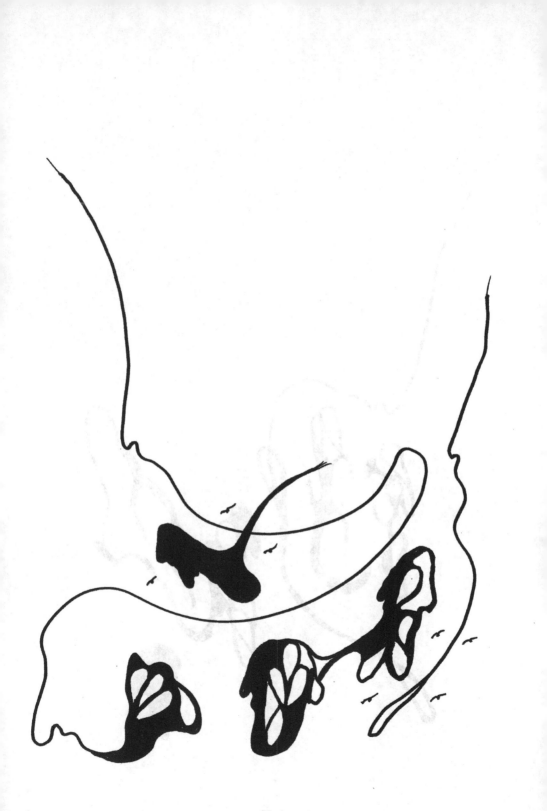

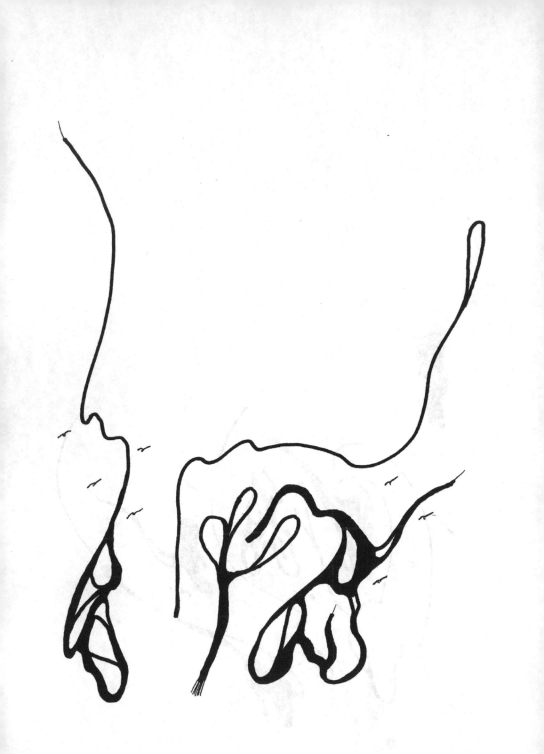

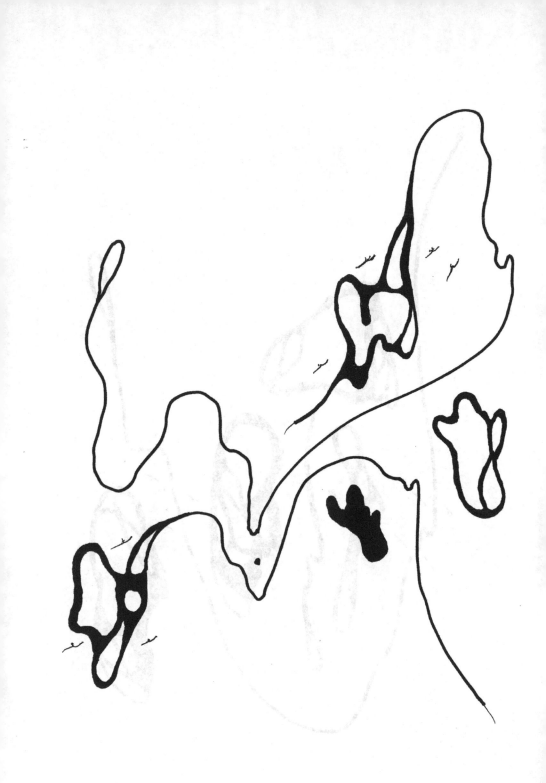

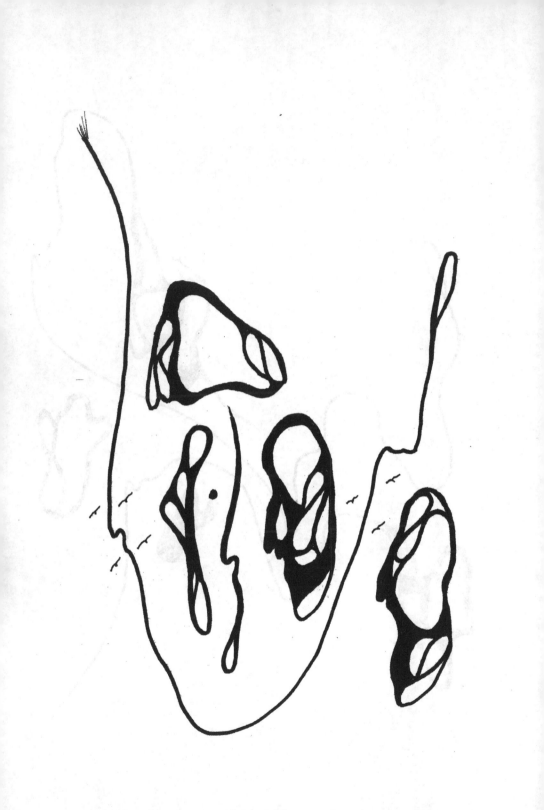

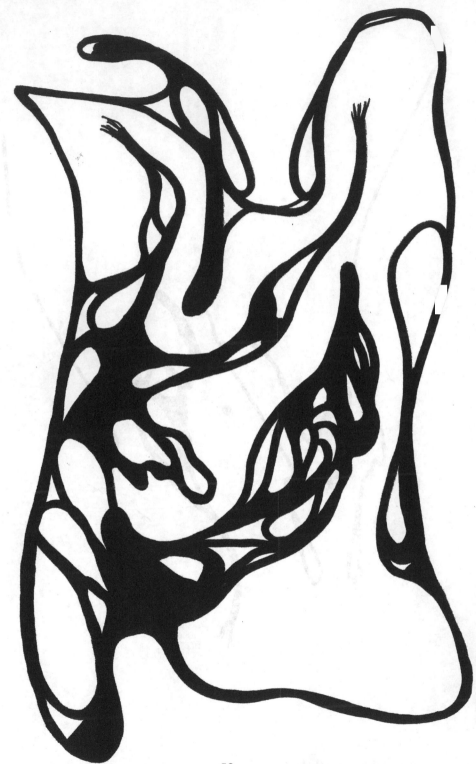

Dedicated
to God and
Jesus Christ
And
in loving
Memory

Of
my

Dad- Mac Bratcher
Mother- Deleta Cox
Stepdad- Roger Neal

"The Lord is gracious, and full of compassion; slow to anger, and of great mercy."

Psalm 145:8